D1208271

Searchlight BOOKS™

Fear Fest

Spine-Tingling Urban Legends

Karen Latchana Kenney

Lerner Publications ◆ Minneapolis

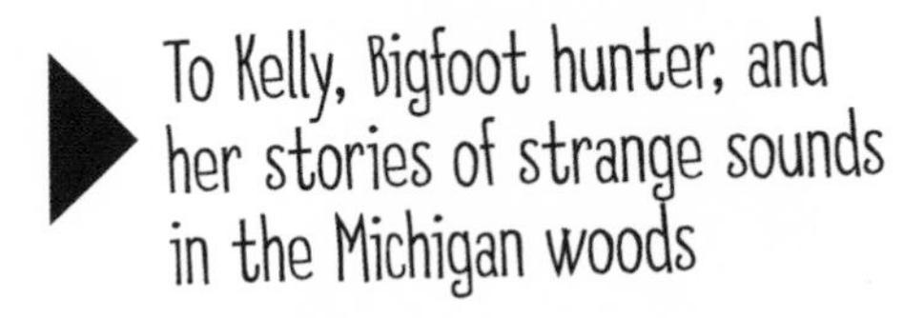

Lerner Publications Company
A division of Lerner Publishing Group, Inc.
241 First Avenue North
Minneapolis, MN 55401 USA

For reading levels and more information, look up this title at www.lernerbooks.com.

Library of Congress Cataloging-in-Publication Data

The Cataloging-in-Publication Data for *Spine-Tingling Urban Legends* is on file at the Library of Congress.
ISBN 978-1-5124-3405-7 (lib. bdg.)
ISBN 978-1-5124-5607-3 (pbk.)
ISBN 978-1-5124-5078-1 (EB pdf)

LC record available at https://lccn.loc.gov/2017002401

Manufactured in the United States of America
1-42041-23911-3/21/2017

Contents

Chapter 1

MYSTERIOUS VISITORS

Imagine your family is driving down a dark and deserted road. Suddenly you see a figure ahead. It's a young woman standing in the beam of the car's headlights. You offer her a ride home, and she climbs into the seat in the far back of your van. But when you arrive at her address, the woman has vanished! At the door, a man tells you she was his daughter. She died five years ago on that very road.

A story about a vanishing woman might be an urban legend. What is an urban legend?

You just met the disappearing hitchhiker. It is one famous urban legend. An urban legend is passed along through stories. It often contains a warning to others. The events include things that could happen to anyone, like driving down a dark road. But then there's a strange or scary twist. The story is told again and again, changing a little as it travels from person to person. It becomes an urban legend that makes you wonder: Did it really happen?

A scary story you hear at a sleepover might be an urban legend.

Watch Out for the Bandage Man!

Some urban legends, like the disappearing hitchhiker, tell of strange people or ghostly visitors. Another legend like this is about a mysterious man in Cannon Beach, Oregon. People call him the Bandage Man. They say he wanders along an old section of road just off Highway 101. The man is wrapped in dirty bandages. His body seems broken, with limbs sticking out in weird ways. People say he tries to jump onto cars that pass by. Maybe it's just a scary story, but locals still avoid driving down that dark road at night for fear of running into the Bandage Man!

Could the bandage man be real? Or is the story just an urban legend?

Fact or Fiction?

Are some urban legends really true?

It's possible!

Many urban legends are believed to be at least partly true, but some are more real than others. For example, there is an urban legend that tells of a couple who checked into a hotel room. During their stay, they noticed a bad smell but did not know what it was. They later found out that a dead body was under the bed the whole time!

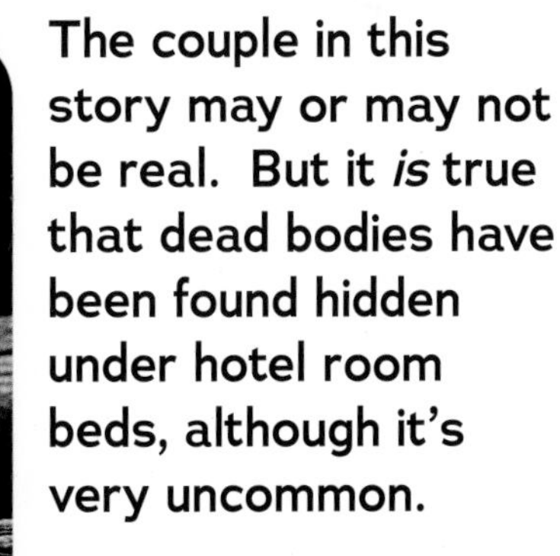

The couple in this story may or may not be real. But it *is* true that dead bodies have been found hidden under hotel room beds, although it's very uncommon.

Many urban legends are said to have happened to a friend's friend. But you are unlikely to actually witness the legend yourself.

Bloody Mary

Have you heard about the legend of Bloody Mary? It describes how to supposedly make the ghost of Bloody Mary appear. You stand in front of a mirror in a dark room, holding a flashlight or a candle. You repeat "Bloody Mary" aloud three times. Then when you look in the mirror, the legend says you will see her ghost. She appears as a woman with a bloody face. Scary!

Bloody Mary is a popular urban legend about a ghost. Can you think of any other ghostly legends?

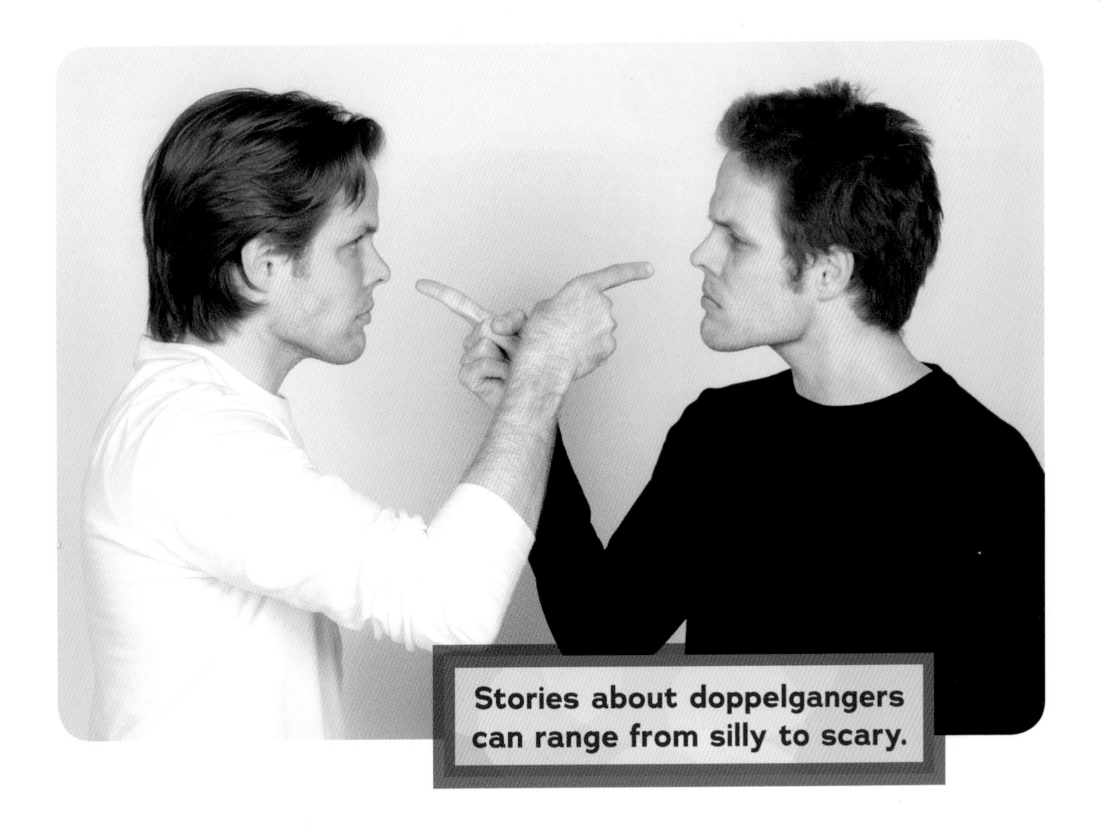

Stories about doppelgangers can range from silly to scary.

Seeing Your Double

Another legend involves seeing a person who looks just like you. This is supposed to be a bad omen. Your double is called a doppelganger. That means "double goer" in German. According to the legend, your doppelganger might be your spirit, separated from your body. Some say England's Queen Elizabeth I saw her doppelganger just before her death in 1603. Of course, other people have reported seeing their doubles too and have been perfectly fine. What do you think?

Chapter 2

CREEPY BUGS

Do bugs scare you? If so, you're not alone. With all their legs and eyes, they can look a little like tiny monsters. They also breed quickly, and then they're crawling everywhere. Just thinking about them can creep you out! It's no wonder bugs are the scary subjects of many urban legends.

Most bugs lay many eggs at a time. What might happen if they lay eggs under someone's skin?

One legend describes a strange spider bite. It is said to have happened to a woman who went on vacation in North Africa. During her trip, she got a few spider bites on her face. When she returned home, the bites got bigger. She was washing her face one morning and felt a prick. Then she watched in horror as hundreds of baby spiders crawled out of her bites. Some even say the woman went crazy from the scary experience!

Spiders lay eggs in sacs filled with hundreds of baby spiders. When the baby spiders come out of their eggs, they break through the sacs and scurry off.

In one legend, getting a haircut is deadly!

Spider in the Hairdo

Imagine getting bugs in your hair! According to the Spider in the Hairdo legend, those bugs could be deadly. The story tells of a California surfer who went to a salon to get his dreadlocks cut. When the stylist cut one especially thick dreadlock, baby black widow spiders crawled out. The story ends with the surfer and stylist dead, killed by the spiders' bites. This story may be freaky, but don't be too scared. While black widow bites harm people, they cannot kill them. You aren't likely to die from a bug hanging out in your hairdo!

A Mysterious Buzzing

Have you heard a strange buzzing in your ear? Or had an unexplainable earache? Some legends say bugs can cause these mysterious conditions. Bugs *can* crawl inside people's ears when they're asleep. In fact, doctors have pulled cockroaches, moths, and more out of ears. It makes the Ants in the Brain legend seem possible. The victim in this story falls asleep next to candy or food. Soon after, the person complains of an itchy face or achy head. The story ends as doctors find ants living inside the person's brain. The bugs made their way in through the person's ear!

The Ants in the Brain legend warns against falling asleep next to sweet treats.

More Than a Sore Eye

One bug legend warns you to never ignore a sore eye. It describes a boy who thought he got dust in his eye. It became sore, so he rubbed it, put eye drops in, and hoped it would get better. But instead, his eye turned red and swollen. Then it got worse. Finally, the boy went to the doctor, who found a live worm just under the boy's eye! Sounds disgusting, right? Still, it has happened. In the late 1990s, doctors pulled the larva of a human botfly from a boy's eye in Honduras. But the chances of this happening again are very slim.

Many things can make your eye sore, but you probably never thought a worm could be the cause!

Fact or Fiction?

Could licking an envelope lead to cockroaches on your tongue?

No!

A well-known story warns against licking envelope glue. In the story, tiny cockroach eggs are stuck in the glue that a woman licks. The eggs stick in a cut on the woman's tongue, and then cockroaches hatch in her mouth. Yuck! Luckily, this isn't true. One flaw in the story is that cockroaches don't lay single eggs. They lay many eggs in an egg case the size of a pea. That would be hard to miss on an envelope!

It's safe to say that a cockroach won't crawl out of your mouth just from licking an envelope.

Chapter 3

MONSTERS AND BEASTS

If tiny insects don't frighten you, how do you feel about larger creatures? Many urban legends are about animals unlike anything you've ever seen. They show up where they don't belong. They might have strange fangs or fur. Some are incredibly large. Urban tales of monsters and beasts may terrify you, but do these strange creatures exist?

People have reported seeing strange monsters almost everywhere. What is one place where a creature is said to live where it doesn't belong?

One scary creature is thought to live in murky city sewers. This urban tale begins with tiny baby alligators. They were once sold as souvenirs to Florida tourists. Once the alligators started growing, their owners lost interest. Some people flushed the alligators down the toilet. That's where the story starts to get strange. Some say that the alligators started living in the New York City sewers. They ate rats and garbage and grew bigger. Although many city officials have said there are no alligators in the sewers, the story keeps spreading.

Have you ever heard about animals living in places where they aren't normally found?

THIS FAMOUS PHOTO STARTED THE LOCH NESS MONSTER LEGEND.

Ancient Survivors?

You never know what lurks in dark, deep waters. Some think that mysterious swimming creatures live in bodies of water around the world. The Loch Ness Monster is one. People have reported seeing this beast rising up from a Scottish lake called Loch Ness. They say it is huge, with a long neck and several humps. People have taken photographs of what they say is the beast. The very first picture of the monster was taken in 1933 but was later proven to be a fake. What do you think?

The Beast of Bodmin Moor

Strange creatures may roam on land too. A legendary beast is said to terrorize Bodmin Moor in Cornwall, England, an open area of land where cattle and sheep graze. People have found livestock ripped apart on the moor. What attacked them? Some believe it is the Beast of Bodmin Moor. It's thought to be catlike with sharp claws, but large wildcats don't normally live in the area. One theory is that the beasts are pumas from a local zoo. Some say the owner released them when the zoo closed in the 1970s. But no one has proof that pumas injured the animals. Is a mysterious beast to blame?

Could the Beast of Bodmin Moor be a puma?

Some say that this is what el Chupacabra looks like.

The Goat Sucker

Another legend comes from Latin and South America. This story features a terrifying beast called el Chupacabra, which means “goat sucker” in Spanish. It attacks livestock, draining sheep, goats, and chickens of their blood from a single wound. Reports of the beast vary. Some say it looks like a mutant coyote or kangaroo. Others say it is lizard-like, with fangs. What is this beast? Nobody has been able to even take a picture of it, but bloodless animal victims still show up.

A Giant Ape?

A different creature is said to lurk in the forests of North America. People report glimpses of an apelike being. It is hairy, huge, and walks on two feet. These creatures are called Bigfoot. A 1967 film shows what many believe to be a female Bigfoot. The footage catches a big, hairy creature crossing a creek. At one point, it turns to look at the camera. Some think these creatures are giant apes called *Gigantopithecus*, which scientists believe are extinct. Could this be what the Bigfoot creatures are? Or is the whole thing a hoax?

Some people believe that this footage from the 1967 film is just a person dressed up in a costume. Others think it is proof that Bigfoot creatures exist.

Fact or Fiction?

Is it true that people go on expeditions to try to find the beasts of urban legends?

Yes!

Groups of people have gone out searching for creatures from famous urban legends. Different organizations take groups of people to remote areas of the United States to look for Bigfoot creatures. The areas are thought to be their habitat zones. These Bigfoot hunters listen for a Bigfoot's call in the woods. They look for large footprints or unusually placed sticks. The Bigfoot hunters collect and study their evidence. They hope to prove Bigfoot creatures really exist.

This Bigfoot hunter holds up a cast of what he thinks is a Bigfoot footprint.

TERRIFYING PLACES

Sometimes urban legends tell about unusual places. These sites might be tombs, bridges, or odd areas of the ocean. They are where people or ships mysteriously disappear. They may be haunted by ghosts or even cursed. Would you dare to visit these terrifying places?

There are many kinds of urban legends. What are some places that might be at the center of urban legends?

Crybaby Bridges

Certain bridges seem to be hot spots of weird activity. Some of these odd bridges are called Crybaby Bridges. People report hearing a baby crying by them, yet no one is around. Legends tell of babies falling to their deaths from the same bridges. Each bridge has a legend of how the babies died. Do the babies' ghosts haunt these bridges?

WOULD YOU DARE TO WALK ON A CRYBABY BRIDGE?

Marie Laveau's tomb is a popular spot for people to test out an urban legend.

The Voodoo Tomb

Cemeteries can be pretty scary places too. One creepy cemetery is in New Orleans. It is called St. Louis Cemetery No. 1, and it has been around since 1789. It contains the voodoo tomb. Buried there is Marie Laveau, who practiced voodoo magic. Many believe that her spirit grants wishes. Visitors must leave gifts of food, money, or flowers at her tomb. Then they have to turn around three times and ask for her help. Lastly, they must mark her tomb with a red *X*.

Mysterious Seas

The Bermuda Triangle seems to make people, planes, and ships vanish. This triangular area is in the ocean between Bermuda, Puerto Rico, and Florida. In December 1945, a group of military planes disappeared there. Their rescue party also disappeared. The planes and their twenty-seven crew members were never found. Other ships and planes have vanished in the area too. Where did they go?

Would you dare to enter the Bermuda Triangle?

Fact or Fiction?

Is it possible that the Bermuda Triangle does more than make planes and boats disappear?

According to legends, yes!

In 1970, Bruce Gernon Jr. described leaping through time while flying over the Bermuda Triangle. During his trip from the Bahamas to Palm Beach, Florida, Gernon said he saw a thick cloud. It surrounded his plane, but he found a clear tunnel to fly through. While he was in the tunnel, the plane sped up and he felt weightless. Then Gernon's plane was out of the cloud and close to Miami. His flight to Florida had taken close to half the time it should have taken. Did he jump through time?

Some believe the fog that Bruce Gernon Jr. flew through had electricity in it that made him travel faster through time.

Can people and even places disappear?

People seem to even disappear from hotel rooms. That's according to the Vanishing Hotel Room legend. It's said that while a woman and her mother were on vacation in another country, the mother became sick. Her daughter left her in the hotel room to get some medicine. When she returned, her mother had vanished. Even the hotel room was missing. Strange! Urban legends like these may or may not be real. Have you heard an urban legend? Think about the details and decide. Can you believe everything you hear?

Believe It or Not!

- People who study legendary creatures are called cryptozoologists. They visit places where the creatures were seen and gather evidence.

- In April 1977, a Japanese fishing ship called *Zuiyo Maru* came across a strange dead creature in the sea. It was 32 feet (9.8 meters) long and had four flippers with a long neck and tail.

- Lake Michigan may have a mysterious triangle just like the Bermuda Triangle. In 1950, a plane vanished while flying over the lake. The plane, its fifty-five passengers, and three crew members have never been found.

Glossary

dreadlock: hair that is grown into a long and thick, ropelike strand

evidence: information and facts that can prove something is true

extinct: no longer living

habitat: a place where something normally lives

hoax: a trick or joke

larva: a young, wormlike form of an insect that hatches from an egg

mutant: a living thing that has different characteristics because of changes in its genes

omen: a sign that something will happen in the future

souvenir: something you buy to remind yourself of a certain place

tourist: a person who travels to another place for fun

Learn More about Urban Legends

Books

Maurer, Tracy Nelson. *Chilling Ancient Curses.* Minneapolis: Lerner Publications, 2018. Read up on even more spooky and scary things that people tell stories about.

McCullum, Kenya. *12 Creepy Urban Legends.* Mankato, MN: 12-Story Library, 2016. Learn about twelve skin-crawling urban legends in this book.

Peabody, Erin. *The Loch Ness Monster.* New York: Little Bee Books, 2017. Find out even more about the great beast at the center of one of the most popular urban legends.

Websites

Discovery Kids: Telltale Sasquatch Signs
http://discoverykids.com/articles/telltale-sasquatch-signs
Read about the signs to look for when searching for Bigfoot creatures, also called Sasquatch.

KidzWorld: Top 5 Halloween Urban Legends
http://www.kidzworld.com/article/26193-top-5-halloween-urban-legends
Learn about some of the most popular scary urban legends.

Science for Kids: The Bermuda Triangle Mystery
http://www.scienceforkidsclub.com/bermuda-triangle.html
Find out the facts about the mysterious Bermuda Triangle.

Index

Photo Acknowledgments

The images in this book are used with the permission of: Lario Tus/Shutterstock.com, p. 4; kryzhov/Shutterstock.com, p. 5; bokan/Shutterstock.com, p. 6; © iStockphoto.com/THEPALMER, pp. 7, 16; Aleshyn_Andrei/Shutterstock.com, p. 8; Radius Images/Alamy Stock Photo, p. 9; © iStockphoto.com/DKart, p. 10; © iStockphoto.com/dennisvdw, p. 11; © iStockphoto.com/ntzolov, p. 12; © iStockphoto.com/Stolk, p. 13; GaevoyB/Shutterstock.com, p. 14; © Anna Peisl/Corbis/Getty Images, p. 15; Richard Levine/Alamy Stock Photo, p. 17; AF archive/Alamy Stock Photo, p. 18; AppStock/Shutterstock.com, p. 19; Alexlky/Shutterstock.com, p. 20; © Bettmann/Getty Images, p. 21; © Vince Talotta/Toronto Star/Getty Images, p. 22; Photosforyou/Alamy Stock Photo, p. 23; Dave Allen Photography/Shutterstock.com, p. 24; © iStockphoto.com/Tiago_Fernandez, p. 25; © iStockphoto.com/DoctorJools, p. 26; Marafona/Shutterstock.com, p. 27; © iStockphoto.com/lolostock, p. 28.

Cover: © Orhan Cam/Shutterstock.com.

Main body text set in Adrianna Regular 14/20.
Typeface provided by Chank.